Sundown Syndrome: The Ultimate Guide to What It Is, Treatment, and Prevention

By: Clayton Geoffreys

Table of Contents

Disclaimer

This book is not intended as a substitute for the medical advice of a physician or medical professional. The reader should regularly visit a doctor in matters relating to his or her health and particularly with respect to symptoms that may require medical diagnosis or attention.

Foreword

Caring for someone with Sundown Syndrome can be difficult and at times overwhelming. Proper education is essential to understanding how to spot symptoms of Sundowner's, how to treat Sundowner's Syndrome, and how to prevent the development of Sundowner's Syndrome in the case where it has not yet begun to develop. There are many different approaches towards treating Sundown Syndrome, and in this book we'll explore several including but not limited to UTIs, medications, and hydration. Later on, we'll learn about ways to deal with early stage Alzheimer's and dementia. Thank you for downloading *Sundown Syndrome: The Ultimate Guide to What It Is, Treatment, and Prevention*. Hope you enjoy and if you do, please do not forget to leave a review! Also, check out my website at claytongeoffreys.com to join my exclusive list where I let you know about my latest books. To thank you for your purchase, you can go to my site to download a free copy of _33 Life Lessons:_ _Success Principles, Career Advice & Habits of_ _Successful People_. In the book, you'll learn from some of the greatest thought leaders of different industries on what it takes to become successful and how to live a great life.

Cheers,

Clayton Geoffreys

Chapter 1: What is Sundown Syndrome?

Alzheimer's disease and dementia exhibit a variety of symptoms, and create challenges and issues for the spouse, other family members, and caregivers. One of those is known as Sundown Syndrome. It's also known as Sundowners, sundowning, and even by some as, "the witching hour." Sundowning is typically defined as increased confusion or anxiety as the day ends or as daylight ebbs. It coincides with the time the body grows more fatigued and tired. In fact, this phenomenon is common among not only those with dementia, but also elderly patients and residents in facilities that do not have a diagnosis of Alzheimer's or other forms of dementia.

Sundown syndrome is also called "spontaneous agitation," and is traditionally caused by over-stimulation, fatigue, and confusion that increase insecurities, restlessness, and disorientation at nighttime. This is believed to be caused by a reduction of visual clues, noises that are familiar and comforting in the daytime, as well as decreased activity.

The term "Sundown" Syndrome is a bit of a misnomer, because it's not classified as a diagnosis, but rather an aspect of behavior that develops in some individuals (but not all) diagnosed with Alzheimer's. In most cases, sundowning occurs during the moderate stage of the condition.

At its most basic definition, as the sun goes down, you may notice that a spouse or family member exhibits certain disruptive behaviors. While this is relatively common to those dealing with moderate to severe stages of Alzheimer's, the symptoms, including agitation, grow worse as darkness falls. While doctors are not quite certain why this occurs or whether it is caused by a change in lighting, or a natural process of growing fatigued and exhausted at the end of the day, this phenomenon is certainly not limited to seniors or those with dementia.

As a matter of fact, 'Sundown Syndrome' can be noticed in young children as well. Have you ever noticed that around dinner time young children, especially those five or younger, grow especially cranky, whiny, or even downright demanding? So in a sense, sundowning is not limited to the elderly population.

Alzheimer's 101

You might say that Alzheimer's disease is generally defined as a progressive, steady loss of mental functions and capabilities caused by degeneration or destruction of brain tissues. This destruction or degeneration also includes loss of nerve cells that often coincide with the development of plaques and neural fiber "tangles" in the brain.

Alzheimer's disease is the most common cause of dementia, accounting for approximately 65% of dementias in the elderly.[1] In fact, the disease affects approximately 1% of individuals between the ages of 60 and 64, and roughly 30% of those over 85 years of age.

Studies have not determined exactly what causes Alzheimer's disease, although it is believed to be somewhat genetic in nature. A working theory is that it is caused by a gene abnormality, including one that affects apolipoprotein E (known as APOE), which identifies the protein portion of some lipoproteins. These lipoproteins are responsible for transporting cholesterol through the bloodstream. The APOE gene is responsible for giving instructions for the synthesis or production of the apolipoprotein E.[2]

Studies have determined that those with APOE e4 allele (or type 4) have an increased risk of developing late onset Alzheimer's disease than others. That is because the APOE e4 allele is involved in the creation of amyloid plaques or clumps of protein often found in the brain of someone diagnosed with Alzheimer's, which contributes to the destruction and death of neurons in the brain. Those with the e2 allele or type 2 seem to be the most resistant against Alzheimer's. However, such genetic testing is not recommended because it is unable to determine whether a person will develop Alzheimer's later in life.

As Alzheimer's progresses parts of the brain literally degenerate. Nerve cells are destroyed, reducing the ability of the remaining nerve cells to respond to chemical messengers (neurotransmitters) that transmit messages or signals. Plaques are defined as clumps of dead nerve cells that contain amyloids, or abnormal and installable proteins. The neuro fiber tangles (neurofibrillary tangles) are defined as literally twisted strands of unstable proteins found in the nerve cell.

Progressive Stages of Alzheimer's

Alzheimer's is broken down into seven stages based on the progression of symptoms. I will briefly cover those to greater understand the point at which Sundown Syndrome may occur.

Stage I

If you or a loved one is not experiencing symptoms or "measurable" cognitive impairment, but you still notice that your cognitive functions or capabilities are slightly 'off', you may not even realize that Alzheimer's is in your future. This stage typically averages one to seven years before you begin to notice worsening symptoms.

Stage II

We are all susceptible to changes in memory or aptitude as we age. We forget where we put things, or have difficulty remembering the names of places or objects. If you do that on a consistent basis, you may be entering into the second stage, or Stage II Alzheimer's. At this point, your doctor or a family member may notice that you're exhibiting mild symptoms, but still with no measurable cognitive impairment.

Stage III

If you're experiencing some measurable cognitive impairment but no functional decline, you may have trouble remembering names or experience more difficulty with otherwise routine tasks. You may

9

experience greater difficulty in organizing or planning things. You are still independent, but may experience mild or minor cognitive difficulties.

Stage IV

If you feel you're struggling more with cognitive changes such as memory lapses, difficulty with language, making poor judgments, and problems with spatial orientation, you may be entering the fourth stage of Alzheimer's. At this point, you may begin to forget incidents in your past, have greater difficulty with mathematical functions, and feel yourself growing moody or challenged by certain situations.

Stage V & VI

You will definitely notice your inability to recall personal historical events, such as where you went to school. Remembering what time of day or even the day of the week becomes more pronounced. While you are still independent in regard to activities of daily living (dressing, taking care of hygiene, toileting) your family may begin to notice behavioral changes. You may feel an increasing sense of aggression, restlessness, apathy, and irritability. At this stage, issues like sundowning or inability to sleep may become more apparent, which will not only increase stress levels on you, but on your loved ones or caregivers.

Stage VII

By this time, you may experience a marked decrease in your ability to remember your personal history, your friends, and even family members. You will need help with dressing, eating, grooming and toileting routines. This stage is defined as severe to end-stage dementia. Bodily functions may begin to cease and create issues of incontinence, falling accidents, and difficulty swallowing. End-stage dementia requires nearly round-the-clock or palliative care.

Is Sundown Syndrome More Common in Certain Types of Dementia?

Sundown Syndrome tends to appear during the moderate stage, and may be noticed as other symptoms and behaviors appear, including wandering, hallucinations, and other behaviors that require more supervision and oversight. The middle stages or Stages V and VI are typically the most common in which Sundown Syndrome, wandering, or increased confusion appear. These stages are also the longest in an Alzheimer's diagnosis, and can last years.

During these two stages, you or a loved one may have more difficulty framing thoughts, communicating, have difficulty dressing and engaging in other "routine" tasks. Behaviors may also become a more noticeable during this stage. Mom may refuse to bathe, for example, or Dad may become verbally aggressive over a perceived slight.

Caregivers may find these stages and changes in behavior some of the most difficult with which to cope. These behavioral changes include constant repetition, eruptions of anger, frequent agitation, confusion, and a number of sleep issues.

The descriptions of stages of Alzheimer's, as well as contributing factors and symptoms, provided by numerous resources such as the Alzheimer's Association are not meant to be super-specific. Characteristics of symptoms and possible behavioral changes, cognitive functioning, and physical abilities classified under different stages is taken from years of observation. They are common, but by no means inclusive. You may experience none of the symptoms in specific stages, or experience them sooner or later throughout the diagnosis and progression of the disease.

The stages as defined are guidelines and provide you, family members and even caregivers with an idea of what can be expected. This does not mean that you will experience those very same symptoms at a specific time. Understanding the basic elements of Alzheimer's disease progression is essential, especially when trying to deal with behavior issues. Because Sundown Syndrome is classified under behavioral issues, it stands to reason that the more you know about it and how it develops, the better equipped you and other family members will be able to deal with it.

Chapter 2: How Does Sundown Syndrome Develop?

According to the Alzheimer's Association, nearly 20% of people diagnosed in various stages of Alzheimer's may begin to experience increased agitation and anxiety as daylight ebbs. Symptoms may also include pacing, disorientation, and increasing levels of confusion. These symptoms often continue through the night, and are classified as "behavioral problems" associated with moderate to severe Alzheimer's diagnoses. Sundowning can increase the risk of injury, so extra oversight is recommended.

Be aware that Sundown Syndrome can erratically disrupt your waking/sleep cycle, which can lead to even more behavioral issues. According to the Alzheimer's Association, Sundown Syndrome as well as other nighttime restlessness or agitation typically "peaks" during the middle stages of the disease process, and then will gradually diminish as you head toward the later stages.

So What Causes Sundowning?

The actual cause of sundown syndrome has not yet been pinpointed, and the behavior affects different people in different ways. However, some of the leading factors that can contribute to sundowning include, but are not limited to:

Fatigue

Alzheimer's can cause extreme physical and mental fatigue for a person striving to make sense of the world around them. The stress placed on the body to deal with confusion, uncertainty, unfamiliarity, and fear takes a great emotional and physical toll. It may also contribute to increased agitation and anxiety by the end of the day.

Reactions of Caregivers and Family

A perceived negative or impatient reaction of your

loved one or a caregiver may contribute to a sense of increased confusion, fear, and frustration for anyone dealing with Alzheimer's. You may already be, and feel increasingly frustrated and tired at the end of the day, but so too are family members or caregivers. A perceived negative reaction, comment, gesture, a look or stance can trigger a negative reaction which initiates a domino-type decline toward evening.

Increasing Darkness

As darkness descends, an increase in shadows may also lead to agitation and anxiety as daylight transitions to evening. Caregivers in long-term care facilities or those working with Alzheimer's patients in clinical settings are often advised not to wear black scrubs or clothing, as some Alzheimer's patients can perceive them as "empty spaces" or "black holes" that cause fear, anxiety, and agitation.

Skewed Reality

As the disease progresses, it becomes increasingly

17

difficult to hang onto reality. It's natural that you or a loved one would grow increasingly disoriented and unable to differentiate between dream states and reality.

Less Need for Sleep

As we grow older, many of us feel like we do not need as much sleep as we used to. This may be due to lack of physical activity or the constant cognitive, reasoning, and rationalizing decisions we had to make when we are working. A person dealing with this situation may begin to stay up later and later, or wake up frequently during the night in a state of confusion. In addition, due to erratic sleep habits depending on physical factors like hunger, pain, or anxiety, a person who awakens numerous times through the night tends to nap frequently throughout the day, sometimes falling asleep constantly through the day with few 'alert' times in between.

According to the *Foundations of Psychiatric Mental*

Health Nursing: A Clinical Approach[3], there can be a reversal of sleep patterns found in the middle stages of Alzheimer's. Many with dementia sleep more during daytime hours than at night. The disease is also known to change normal sleep cycles, reducing rapid eye movement or REM sleep.

Not only that, but sleep deprivation can eventually lead to delusions and hallucinations. Often, in the case of Alzheimer's, such symptoms are utilized in the diagnostic criteria for a number of psychiatric disorders including anxiety, manic episodes, as well as major depressive disorders.

A progression in the severity of sleeping/waking disturbances can lead to a disruption of circadian rhythm sleep. A circadian rhythm sleep disorder is defined as a recurrent or persistent disruption in the pattern of sleep that can result in the altered function of our circadian "timing system." It may also result in confusion between an individual's natural circadian sleeping/waking cycle and external physical demands.

In order to track the development of Sundown Syndrome symptoms, doctors often recommend that family members or caregivers keep a journal or diary. Write down the time of day, the situation, and what is happening before a sundowning episode occurs in order to help you identify the trigger or the situation that initiated the Sundown Syndrome behaviors. By jotting down these incidents, you can help to avoid such incidents or triggers in the future.

Circadian rhythm and over-stimulation may be major contributing factors that initiate or trigger numerous Sundown Syndrome symptoms, but again, each person reacts to stimulus or external environment changes differently. For example, something as innocuous as a radio playing too loud can trigger a downward spiral into negative behaviors in the evening. Please note, however, that just because you get more irritable in the evening that you necessarily have Sundown Syndrome.

Take into consideration a number of additional factors that may be causing a negative reaction or behavior in yourself or a loved one. Such issues may involve:

- Pain
- Level of comfort
- Digestion issues
- Needing to use the bathroom
- Hunger or thirst
- Depression
- Frustration

As you can see, the reasons for why Sundown Syndrome occurs are not only physical in nature, but frequently emotional as well. That said, you may notice that you or your loved one only experiences or exhibits some of the symptoms of Sundown Syndrome once in a while or quite infrequently. Always try to determine what has triggered the episode. Do not think that because it happens once in a while that such occurrences will occur nightly.

Like other aspects of the disease process, incidents may come and go, stick around for a few days (or weeks) and then disappear. If you believe that you're dealing with (and you're trying to cope with) Sundown Syndrome, schedule a visit with your doctor and try to get to the root of the problem.

In many cases, Sundown Syndrome may be triggered by disruption of the circadian rhythm that most of us rely on to tell us when it is time to go to bed and when it is time to get up. In most cases, that refers to sunrise and sunset. In the history of man, hunting and gathering was done during the day and for centuries people went to bed shortly after the sun set. Today, with more convenient lifestyles and technologies that encourage us to stay up later (have to watch the eleven o'clock news before I go to bed!) that rhythm may be altered.

A proper toileting schedule is also recommended. Take care of toileting promptly or following a schedule to ensure you or your loved one gets to the bathroom every two to three hours as needed. It is recommended that toileting take place shortly before bedtime in order to reduce discomfort or the need to get up soon after you fall asleep. In addition, make sure that pain management needs are being monitored and dealt with in a timely manner. Some medications must be taken with food, so talk to your doctor about timing of medications to ensure that discomfort is eliminated or at least reduced during the nighttime sleep hours.

As we age, and depending on external physical conditions (disease, pain, and hunger/thirst), these rhythms may grow even more out of whack. You or a loved one diagnosed with dementia may toss and turn all night and nap all day. Understanding this cycle is important in reducing symptoms of Sundown

Syndrome.

Chapter 3: Understanding Circadian Rhythms

Understanding circadian rhythms is essential in understanding Sundown Syndrome and a potential cause. The National Institutes of Health[4] define circadian rhythms as behavioral changes that may involve aspects of physical as well as mental behaviors that occur on a 24-hour basis. In most cases, our personal circadian rhythm is based on aspects of daylight and nighttime. For example, we are up and working during the daytime hours, and tend to slow down, relax, and sleep during nighttime hours.

Circadian rhythms can also be observed in nature - a flower closes its petals at night and then opens them up at dawn. Circadian rhythm is not the same as a "biological clock", but the two are linked together. In essence, our "biological clocks" manipulate circadian rhythms based on the interaction of cellular structures in our body. Sunlight and nightfall determine certain output or rhythms produced in the suprachiasmatic nucleus of the brain.

This cluster of approximately 20,000 nerve cells is found in the hypothalamus, which is a very important gland that regulates and monitors a variety of body conditions. The hypothalamus sends signals to the brain's thinking center, the cortex, which determines our actions. A great majority of the regulatory or functional work of the brain goes on in the cortex, monitored by the hypothalamus.

Even in spite of work environments (such as individuals who worked the graveyard shift), our circadian rhythms are set, to a certain point, and are genetically inherited. For example, if a child's parent or both parents tend to be "night people" and stay up later at night and get up later in the morning, those children may very well develop the same type of circadian rhythm or sleep pattern. While most of us do not have much control over our circadian rhythms, they can be affected by our environment.

At its most basic definition, our circadian rhythms are responsible for maintaining our body temperature, the release of hormones, and heavily influence our sleeping/waking patterns or cycles. These rhythms are naturally linked to a variety of sleep disorders, including insomnia, as well as other medical conditions including depression, Seasonal Affective Disorder (SAD), diabetes, and obesity.

How Do Circadian Rhythms Work?

In regards to sleep, your circadian rhythm, or to be more specific, the suprachiasmatic nucleus, determines and controls the synthesis or manufacturing of melatonin levels in the body. Melatonin is a hormone that makes us feel sleepy.

According to dementia.org,[5] lack of sleep and lack of sleep quality can lead to fatigue and even exhaustion.

This mental state enhances and can exacerbate states of confusion for those in the moderate stages of Alzheimer's.

It is believed that an increase in protein plaques associated with Alzheimer's can create chaos or initiate 'traffic' within the suprachiasmatic nucleus in the brain. These changes are triggered by sensory cues including the light and darkness.

As circadian rhythm and disruption and Sundown Syndrome occur during the middle stages of Alzheimer's, confusion increases. Very often, the person with Alzheimer's senses this greater awareness of confusion, leading to frustration, impatience, and agitation. Mood swings and irritability are most commonly observed by spouses, family members, or caregivers at this time. In fact, Alzheimer's patients dealing with circadian rhythm disruption may experience an increase in their tendency to pace and even wander due to their restlessness.

It should be noted that wandering, reduced sleep time at night, and daytime napping are very common in Alzheimer's as the disease progresses and other forms of dementia as well. Before turning to prescription medications, a number of alternative suggestions for preventing Sundown Syndrome might help.

However, when broaching the topic of prescription sleep aids with your doctor, it is important to determine the overall efficacy of that medication. Some medications exacerbate unsteadiness, agitation, or confusion. That is because those diagnosed with most forms of dementia are very sensitive to medications, especially those that have sedative effects. For this reason, when talking to a doctor about prescription medications to enhance sleep, he or she typically recommends starting out at the lowest possible dose that provides effective results.

Keep in mind that if you're dealing with someone diagnosed with Alzheimer's who is already experiencing Sundown Syndrome or other symptoms associated with a disruption of the circadian rhythm cycles, and is taking anti-anxiety or other sedative type medications, combining them with a medication that increases sleep potentially may exacerbate symptoms.

Some of the most common sleep aids recommended for those dealing with Sundown Syndrome or destruction of circadian rhythms include benzodiazepines. This classification or group of drugs can include but is not limited to:

- Ativan - lorazepam
- Xanax – alprazolam
- Klonopin – clonazepam
- Valium – diazepam
- Restoril - temazepam

However, the above prescription medications are often avoided by doctors because they can make confusion and forgetfulness worse. They are also cautious in prescribing such medications because they can increase risk of falls as well as dependency.

Many caregivers get so desperate for a good night sleep that they resort to over-the-counter medications to help their loved one's sleep. One of the most common is Benadryl. However, while it is not habit forming, Benadryl will interact with a variety of other medications and can make unsteadiness and confusion worse. Benadryl can also contribute to urinary retention and constipation and should not be used in anyone diagnosed with glaucoma.

Sleep aids such as Lunesta or Ambien may be prescribed, with dosage averaging between 1 to 2 mg for the elderly, but such medications may also lead to dependence. A relatively new sleep aid on the market today - Rozerem (ramelteon) - may also lead to physical dependence.

Chapter 4: The Most Common Sundown Syndrome Symptoms

You may notice that toward the end of the day, you or your loved one grows increasingly agitated, one of the most observable and noticeable symptoms of Sundown Syndrome. Recognizing such symptoms is important, not only when making efforts to reduce agitation at the end of the day, but in providing quality, compassionate, and understanding care.

Family members or caregivers can be extremely challenged by a number of not only cognitive, but behavioral changes in a loved one when diagnosed with Alzheimer's. These changes are often difficult enough to deal with without adding other symptoms common to sundowning that may occur toward the moderate to early late stages of the disease process.

In this section, I will mention seven of the most common Sundown Syndrome symptoms so that you know what to watch out for and prepare yourself and other family members) in which they live to reduce severity. When a caregiver or family member recognizes some of the symptoms of sundowning, it is time to take steps to reduce incidents or triggers that initiate the behaviors, which better serves everyone involved.

Irritability and agitation is nothing new to any one of us, especially after a long day at work, school, or taking care of family responsibilities and obligations. We all feel this way at times, but when coupled with cognitive decline, limited mobility, and lack of control over our environment, you can imagine that it would be quite easy to become frustrated or agitated with our environment. This is true of someone experiencing Sundown Syndrome. A person with Sundown Syndrome may grow increasingly agitated and irritable toward late afternoon and during the evening hours. What causes this onset of agitation?

A number of factors may be responsible for this increased sense of agitation, including but not limited to:

- Weariness or exhaustion
- Too much stimulation at the end of the day
- Inadequate lighting

Additional common symptoms include:

- Pacing/restlessness
- Wandering (mild to moderate)
- Rocking
- Stubbornness/Verbal abuse/Anger
- Radical mood swings
- Crying

As long as the environment is safe and well lit, it is often best to let the individual pace, which may help to reduce restlessness and an increasing sense of agitation. Another common symptom of Sundown Syndrome is known as "shadowing" and is similar to pacing. In such instances, your loved one may literally follow you from room to room (even into the bathroom) as if they are afraid of being left alone even for a moment. During this shadowing, he or she may constantly ask you questions, and even though you answer them, those questions will be repeated over, and over, and over again.

Wandering is also relatively common, and your loved one may try to open doors or get into places (such as the garage) that may pose dangers to your loved one such as gasoline, gardening tools and equipment, and so forth. In such cases, safeguard your loved one by installing locks up high, or even disguising outside doors to prevent wandering outside - especially in inclement weather.

In regard to verbal abuse, stubbornness, and accusations often leveled at caregivers by an individual with Alzheimer's, such behaviors may be exacerbated with Sundown Syndrome. A person with Alzheimer's is no longer "grounded" or dealing with reality, and their beliefs, as far as they are concerned, are honest and true. At times, they may believe that someone is stealing from them (including you) or that you are doing something that is hurtful/harmful to them. Such accusations may contribute to some hoarding behaviors, but in many cases can be dealt through simple reassurance. Avoid arguing or consistently denying the accusation, because it may only lead to confrontation and increased agitation responses. Try not to take such accusations personally. If Mom thinks you have stolen her jewelry, calmly show her where it is. The same goes for food, money, or favorite belongings.

You may notice your loved one sitting in a chair, rocking forward and backward. They may also engage in hand-wringing while they are rocking. This is often an indication that something is going on at the moment to cause an increase in anxiety. Do the best you can to determine what is causing the anxiety and then calm and reassure them. Singing, putting on music, or turning the television on with low volume, suggesting a walk, or asking for "help" with a household task is often beneficial in distracting them.

In other cases, you may notice that your loved one is experiencing a wider range and frequency of mood changes during late afternoon and early evening. They are perfectly content and pleasant one minute, and crying the next. This is also relatively common. As a family member and/or caregiver, your main task is to reassure the individual that they are safe. Do what you can to restore some stability, or use distraction/diversion to try to pull them away from their fears and get them engaged in something that is calming to their emotions.

In such situations, it's extremely important to maintain a sense of calmness as much as possible. Remember that an individual with Alzheimer's, and one experiencing the symptoms of Sundown Syndrome, is very adept at "sensing" or reading someone else's emotions. A sigh of frustration, a roll of the eyes, or a slightly raised voice can trigger increased agitation and fearfulness.

Depending on the level of agitation, and the acceleration symptoms, an individual with Sundown Syndrome may also experience more severe symptoms which can include:

- Aggression/Violence
- Hallucinations
- Paranoia
- "Panicked" wandering

Let's talk a moment about "panicked" wandering situations. This describes a situation where the individual "must get to the train" even though they have not worked in 10 or 20 years and it's the middle of the night, or "must go pick up the kids from school" even though the kids are grown now with children of their own.

Be aware that in such situations, the person is convinced that they are right, and it can be extremely difficult to defuse such situations. This occurs not only in family caregiving situations, but in professional facilities. At times, these individuals can become so agitated that they get violent. They may curse, lash out, and even try to hit, spit, or scratch their caregivers or family members.

Such situations are extremely painful for family members to watch, but try to imagine the sense of panic of the person experiencing that overwhelming need or desire. That older woman is panicking because she thinks her kids are going to be left alone and vulnerable if she does not get to the school to pick them up on time! Grandpa may honestly feel that if he does not get to work, he'll lose his job.

That being said, this degree of agitation often builds up gradually through the evening, so taking steps to prevent it from getting to that level is up to the family member or caregiver who is/are required to observe when changes in mood or other behavior patterns begin to decline.

Watching for Signs

Watch for signs of an impending outburst or increasing agitation. Yes, some occur without warning, but others are the result of slowly built-up agitation. If you sense an outburst is on the verge, try diversions or distractions. Offer your loved one something to eat, take them for a quick walk outside, or put on some favorite music. Giving them something to do with their hands may also be beneficial.

If you have noticed that Mom or Dad gets increasingly agitated and violent at bath time, for example, you may need to get help with the bathing process and take care of such tasks earlier in the morning rather than waiting until afternoon or evening.

Staying Safe during an Outburst

If you find yourself dealing with a violent outburst, take a number of precautions to ensure that not only your loved one, but everyone is protected. For example, if you have noticed that violent outbursts are more frequent and severe, you may need to take steps to "safeguard" the home environment. You may need to relocate objects that can be easily picked up and thrown. Avoid turning your back to the individual, and try to stay at least an arm's length away while at the same time trying to distract or divert their attention to something else. Speak in a calm and reassuring tone of voice to hide your sense of fear or panic from the individual, which can often just make it worse.

In a home based care scenario, it's also advisable to have the phone number of other family members and friends as well as emergency first responders on hand in case things get out of control and you are concerned not only for the safety of your loved one, but yourself or other family members. That being said, it's important to remember that your loved one is not behaving in such a way because they want to hurt you. Try not to take such behaviors or anything said in such situations personally. In many cases, not only do they not know what they are saying, but after the episode is over, they will not remember having said it.

Situations like this can be extremely emotional and heartbreaking for caregivers, especially for family members who provide care.

Chapter 5: How to Prevent Sundown Syndrome from Developing

It should be understood in no uncertain terms that a cognitive disease process like Alzheimer's cannot – at this time – be prevented. That goes for the range of emotional and physical symptoms and behaviors that come along with that diagnosis – including Sundown Syndrome. As mentioned in the beginning of this guide, this cluster of behavior is just that – behaviors that are sometimes associated with Alzheimer's.

Some people may experience symptoms or behaviors associated with sundowning while others will not. For some, the symptoms are temporary and are alleviated with simple remedies like altering schedules, while for others, the symptoms or behaviors may last weeks, months, or even years.

Sundown Syndrome does not affect everyone diagnosed with Alzheimer's, but it's best to be prepared if it does. Again, it's impossible to say how severe or how long the symptoms or behaviors will last. However, it is not permanent. Observations have shown that as the disease progresses toward the later stages, the symptoms of Sundown Syndrome diminish.

Various stages of the Alzheimer's or dementia disease process provoke a variety of behaviors in some individuals, while not in others. It is difficult to predict how any one person is going to react to the development of the disease, physically or cognitively. While it is not actually possible to "prevent" Sundown Syndrome, caregivers can take steps to reduce the number of triggers or circumstances that typically initiate some of the most common behaviors of the syndrome. When it comes to Sundown Syndrome, understanding and recognizing the potential triggers or cause-and-effect scenarios may help to prevent or reduce the frequency and severity of symptoms, some of which were mentioned in the previous section.

Sundown Syndrome, in addition to increasing agitation, confusion, and fear in an individual, may also progress into repetitive behaviors and questions, physical aggression, and wandering. Because many of the symptoms of Sundown Syndrome are caused by the physical and mental fatigue of dealing with limited mobility, cognitive impairment, and anxiety felt and experienced by the individual with Alzheimer's all day long, it stands to reason that tackling some of the issues most common to blame for this increased agitation during the late afternoon and evening hours may help reduce and even prevent some from occurring.

Exercise and Mobility

In some cases of Sundown Syndrome, constant napping throughout the day increases the potential that the individual will not be tired at night, increasing situations of restlessness, sleeplessness, and a tendency to resist an otherwise 'normal' nighttime sleep cycle.

To reduce this tendency, you should try to promote various types of activity through the day and discourage napping or inactivity.

This is not to imply that you need to keep a loved one constantly moving, but reduce nap times to one hour at most, and try to encourage those naps early in the afternoon. If the individual does not want to nap, encourage 'quiet time' or 'downtime', such as listening to quiet music, looking out a window, or just visiting quietly. Keep in mind that individuals with Alzheimer's can only tolerate a certain amount of stimulus. Toward the end of the day, try to reduce the amount of stimulation from external environments (children, radio, or too many things going on at once).

Some suggestions for exercise and activity include walks, social interaction (but not over-stimulating interaction), encouragement to help with household tasks, continuing (whenever possible based on cognitive ability) to maintain skills and hobbies, and anything else that enhances brain functions. Physical exercise also promotes exercise to the brain through sensory input – whether it's a short walk around the back yard or around the block.

Lighting

I have briefly commented about having adequate lighting and lights on in the house as afternoon transitions into evening. However, light therapy may help to reduce severity and frequency of symptoms associated with Sundown Syndrome. For example, caring.com recommends placing a person who experiences symptoms of Sundown Syndrome near a full spectrum fluorescent lamp for two hours every morning, which is believed to help restore circadian rhythm, or that "biological clock," as well as help reduce agitation. The recommendation is to place the person approximately three feet away from a lamp (2,500 to 5,000 lux).

Why is light important? Some studies have determined that an Alzheimer's patient may only be exposed to bright light approximately 30 minutes a day, while an individual living in the long-term care facility or nursing home may not be exposed to any bright light above 2,000 lux, and may only be exposed to approximately 1,000 lux for 10 to 20 minutes daily! Light is at the basis of circadian rhythm, as well as its positive impact on mood and sight.

Routines

Routines can help prevent and/or lessen some symptoms of Sundown Syndrome. For example, a person with Alzheimer's may become agitated or fearful, and express confusion and other behaviors due to unexpected events during the day. Such events include visitors that he or she does not recognize, or even does not like for whatever reason. Whenever possible, schedule visitors during a time of day when your loved one is more alert, or more easily distracted or diverted. Try to maintain regular routines which can help to reduce incidents of confusion or agitation. These routines provide a sense of stability to those diagnosed with Alzheimer's and other forms of dementia.

Routines are especially important when it comes to bedtime. Set a routine for bedtime and stick to it. For example, going to bed at the same time every night, and developing a routine, such as a back rub, a glass of warm milk, reading out loud, praying, or singing a song quietly just before bedtime. This routine promotes a calm atmosphere. You may even promote a greater sense of calmness by offering a stuffed animal or even a pet that may provide a soothing, calming, sleeping environment for the individual.

White Noise

Some form of "white noise" may help to induce sleep and provide reassurance. White noise can be anything from soft music to gadgets that play the sound of birds chirping, ocean waves, rain, or other type of gentle background noise. Sometimes even the whir of a fan can promote better sleep and provide a constant sense of calmness to those who have difficulty falling asleep. White noise also helps encourage the individual to fall back asleep if they wake up in the middle of the night.

"Go With the Flow"

This is certainly not a scientific term or approach, but it may help to relieve agitation, especially in more severe cases of symptoms associated with Sundown Syndrome that include getting up multiple times during the night and wandering. An individual may get up during the night if he or she feels hungry or thirsty. For example, a loved one who often wakes during the night because they are hungry may benefit from a small plate or dish of peeled orange sections, kiwi or other preferred fruit by the bedside. Of course, always make sure that the individual does not have any swallowing problems and will not choke on these foods. Such an approach may reduce the person's desire to get up out of bed to find something to eat, and they may fall back to sleep faster and easier.

Toileting

Toileting just before bedtime is encouraged to reduce instances of an individual having to get up and go to the bathroom in the middle of the night numerous times. Because the individual may "wake up" more fully by having to walk or navigate a room or hallway to get to the bathroom, it is encouraged that a bedside commode be placed next to the bed to facilitate toileting efforts if needed.

Be aware that toileting may become more challenging as Alzheimer's stages progress. Continence may become an issue. In such cases, protect bedding by using special pads to protect the mattress. Check for dryness frequently in order to prevent development of skin issues like redness, irritation, blistering or decubitus ulcers caused by constant contact with urine or feces. Protect the skin whenever possible by using moisture barriers in situations where incontinence is an issue.

When it comes to reducing or preventing Sundown Syndrome from developing, the key is consistency. When you find something that works, keep doing it. Explore options and try to find different ways to reduce episodes caused by triggers. Do what you can to keep your loved one safe. Comfort, safety, and a sense of security go a long way in reducing the severity and frequency of Sundown Syndrome symptoms.

Chapter 6: What Can Caregivers do to Help Cope with Sundown Syndrome?

As you head closer to the middle stages of Alzheimer's, the focus of care gradually shifts from the person diagnosed and more onto family members and/or caregivers. This is not to imply that you will not be able to participate in your own care, but you may feel more challenged in doing so. As the symptoms worsen and cognitive abilities decline, this stage is something that you and your family should be prepared for. There will be times when you have increased difficulty with dressing, hygiene, and controlling your mental thoughts and physical actions.

Coping with any aspect of Alzheimer's or other forms of dementia is challenging for loved ones and caregivers. This is especially true in cases where Sundown Syndrome develops. Providing care on a 24-hour basis is exhausting enough for most caregivers without having to face challenges of sundowning. Coping with frustration, stress, fatigue, and the need to be available 24/7 are the most common issues that a family caregiver faces. Utilizing a number of suggestions by the Alzheimer's Association may help caregivers cope.

The organization provides a variety of tips and strategies to help deal with this aspect of a dementia diagnosis. For example, one of the most important things for caregivers to always remember is to take care of yourself. When you are tired, exhausted, frustrated, or impatient, those feelings not only have an effect on your emotional, mental, and physical health and well-being, but can exacerbate trigger reactions in a loved one. This increases agitation and confusion in the Alzheimer's patient. If necessary, find someone (a family member, a professional caregiver, a friend) who can provide you with an emotional outlet.

Do Not Feel Guilty About Your Emotions

For many, caregiving is an extremely rewarding endeavor, and we may have a passion for it, but at the same time, we're only human. Be aware of your physical, mental, and emotional limitations. When you need a break, step back and take a break. Only when you are rested, refreshed, and have a positive attitude can you continue to provide safe, compassionate, and high-quality care. For this reason, it is important to find someone who can step in to give you a break once in a while.

When you are dealing with someone with Sundown Syndrome, it's especially important to take regular breaks and step away from the situation if you can, at least for an hour or two every day. Even ten-minute breaks every hour or so can help relieve tension. In some cases, this is just not possible, so try to get as much rest at night as you can. In some cases, you may need to resort to napping when your loved one naps during the day, as is common for individuals with Sundowners. This is not ideal, but do what you can to rest, refresh, and rejuvenate your mind and body when you can.

Pay Attention to Signs or Triggers

An individual experiencing the increased agitation or restlessness of Sundown Syndrome may find that a calmer atmosphere or environment may help reduce symptoms. For example, if the individual with Alzheimer's lives in a busy family environment, in which the evening hours tend to be busier, with children home, the TV on, the activity of preparing dinner, and so forth, this can all create stress. In such cases, maintaining a calm and quiet environment can be quite challenging, and at times, unreasonable, at least for other family members. However, this additional activity and noise can increase confusion, agitation, impatience, and sometimes even aggression for a person in the moderate stages of Alzheimer's or one that experiences sundowning.

Explore options to deal with such a situation. For example, do what you can to reduce how much activity is going on at any given time, or try to relocate the individual to a quieter area of the house during this busy time. No doubt about it, this is an extremely challenging situation, but through trial and error, you can make an effort to reduce the amount of external stimulation that may also lead to reduction of negative behaviors.

The more active (without over-stimulation) the person experiencing Sundown Syndrome can be or the more exercise a person can get throughout the day, the more likely they will be ready to rest at night. Take care of errands, doctor's appointments, or other needs of the person in the morning or early afternoon hours to help avoid that increasing sense of agitation that occurs later in the day.

Clearly Delineate Daytime and Nighttime Hours

For example, toward late afternoon, you might close curtains and turn on lights in the house to reduce signs of agitation. Keep lights on until bedtime, which may help to establish a set routine for awake/sleep time for the individual as well as help to reestablish optimal circadian rhythm.

Individuals experiencing Sundown Syndrome tend to pace because they're restless. As long as the individual is within a safe environment, do not try to restrict this pacing, as it can only lead to irritation, and sometimes even violent outbursts. This is another good reason to keep the interior of the home well lit. If possible, and when weather permits, take the individual outdoors for a little walk. This serves not on as a distraction, but exercise that helps promote rest and sleep.

Plan Activities Early on in the Day to Decrease Agitation

One of the biggest challenges for caregivers in taking care of someone with Sundown Syndrome is with hygiene. You may notice, after a few misguided attempts, that suggesting or trying to encourage a loved one to take a bath or shower later in the day or before bed is nothing but a struggle. Instead, offer showering, washing hair, bathing, clipping fingernails and toenails, and other aspects of personal care in the morning hours.

When people are being taken care of on a daily basis, they get used to being taken care of. At times, when a caregiver or a family member needs to deal with something else, the person with Alzheimer's may become agitated because the focus of attention has shifted from them to that other something. If you have certain tasks to do such as the dishes, business tasks or school homework or studying, or you are just trying to sit down and read for a few minutes, giving the person something to do will also keep them occupied. Like what?

Always suggest activities that you know that they are cognitively able to do. For example, can they help fold some towels? Sort blue (or any other color) buttons/marbles/thread spools out of a box of buttons/marbles/thread spools? Can they "dry" silverware that they can then put in a basket (without sorting)? The key is to give them something to do that will not only distract them, but encourage them to feel as if they are being productive and help you accomplish something. At other times, another family member can step in to give you a break.

Do Not Try to Convince or Argue with Your Loved One That Something Is Not What It Appears

For example, inadequate lighting in a household can cause confusion, agitation, and sometimes even fear. They may see things that are not there, or imagine things that are, especially in dark spaces and shadowed corners. That is another reason to ensure that the home or environment is well lit.

Try to use reassuring and positive statements in a calm tone of voice if the person starts growing agitated. When possible, try to encourage them away from the area that is causing them concern. Never pull, tug, or yank on the person. This can quickly devolve into a volatile and abusive situation. Avoid arguing or raising your voice. Instead, try to distract them. Put on soft music that you know they will like, or a television channel that may distract them. Give them something to do with their hands, which is also often effective.

Always remember that in the mind of a person with Alzheimer's, everything is confusing. This confusion can be exhausting. By the end of the day, they are at their wits' end. Remember that they do not want to feel like this. Their confusion, agitation, and inability to control their emotions, express themselves, or even to do the simplest tasks is extremely frustrating and aggravating. Inside, they are panicking, wanting only to have the control they used to have.

When you find yourself getting frustrated with any aspects of Alzheimer's, and most especially Sundown Syndrome, remember to stop, relax, and put yourself in the shoes of that individual. It's scary! A person who's terrified inside is not going to rationalize that a nighttime bath might help make them feel more relaxed so that they can sleep. Be a compassionate, caring, and understanding caregiver. Use your imagination and try to come up with ways that work in your specific situation. They may not work all the time, but reducing agitation and severity of Sundown Syndrome symptoms is not only beneficial to the individual, but to their caregivers and family members.

Chapter 7: The 9 Actionable Steps to Treating Sundown Syndrome

One of the most beneficial ways to 'treat' Sundown Syndrome is to reduce triggers. Keep a journal or a log to determine what types of things trigger initiation of Sundown Syndrome in your loved one or the person you are caring for. Then take steps to try to eliminate or at least reduce such instances. Keep in mind that fear and anxiety may increase later in the day and altered perceptions and even sometimes hallucinations can come into play. When a person experiences Sundown Syndrome, he or she may also experience a reaction to sensory stimulus. Their perceptions change. For example, a person may suddenly believe that the drapery pull cord is a snake.

1. Nutrition

Nutrition is essential in helping to prevent a number of the symptoms associated with Sundown Syndrome.

For example, studies have explored the theory that some individuals are susceptible to the syndrome because they may be hungry. Hunger can cause physical discomfort. They may experience a drop in blood pressure after eating. This drop in blood pressure reduces the amount of blood that reaches the brain. Erratic blood sugar levels can promote confusion and agitation, just as they do for someone with diabetes if their insulin levels are not adequately maintained. Encourage and offer light snacking through the day. Fruits such as apples can help to replace lost stores of energy.

Reduce gastrointestinal discomfort and/or encourage relaxation by serving the main meal in the middle of the day and having a smaller and simpler meal for dinner or supper time. For example, in the evening, serving soup and sandwich combinations or smaller, more easily digestible foods that does not leave a person with a full stomach may also relieve some triggers that initiate sundowning behaviors.

2. Deal with Vision or Hearing Issues

An individual with hearing or vision problems may also experience more behaviors with Sundown Syndrome as light changes around them. Ensure that your loved ones have access to regular vision and hearing appointments that promote the use of eyeglasses and/or hearing aids when needed to help reduce the sense of confusion as night falls. Individuals diagnosed with macular degeneration may see shadows where no shadows exist. Even the light shining through the blinds can create shadows or "images" that a person diagnosed with Alzheimer's as well as vision problems may believe are "strangers in the house." Again, it's all about perception.

3. Hydration

It is imperative to avoid dehydration, which can cause reduced sensory perception as well as increase confusion, and for some, hallucinations in an individual with Alzheimer's. This may be extremely challenging, because many people with Alzheimer's do not want to drink adequate amounts of water throughout the day. In such situations, try encouraging a loved one to suck on popsicles. Avoid caffeine - this may seem like a no-brainer, but try to avoid and encourage the individual not to smoke or drink (this may be challenging, depending on the prior lifestyle and habits of the individual). Anything with caffeine should be avoided within several hours of bedtime.

4. UTIs

Urinary tract infections may also promote symptoms that are similar to Sundown Syndrome, but are something totally different. A UTI can trigger abrupt mood and behavior changes in any elderly individual, let alone one diagnosed with Alzheimer's or another form of dementia. Urinary tract infections are most commonly caused by dehydration, but may also be associated with heart or liver disease, kidney disease, as well as diabetes. If your loved one or the person you are caring for has been diagnosed any of the listed conditions, make sure they stay hydrated.

5. Reduce Pain Levels

Pain in elderly patients diagnosed with Alzheimer's or other forms of dementia may experience Sundown Syndrome symptoms due to pain. Pain can cause not only sleeplessness, but agitation. This is especially common in those diagnosed with arthritis, one who chronically experiences constipation, or someone who has been sitting in a chair all day, especially if they are uncomfortable. In some cases where patients take medications, the medications may wear off toward the late afternoon and early evening, increasing discomfort levels and exacerbating behaviors caused by pain that may be mistaken for Sundown symptoms. In some cases, some medications may actually exacerbate Sundown Syndrome symptoms.

6. Medications

Depending on the severity of the symptoms, a doctor may recommend medications to relieve agitation during the late afternoon and early evening hours. This topic will be discussed more fully in an upcoming section. Be aware that prescription medications do offer benefits, but many also have drawbacks. If you feel that medications are warranted for your loved one due to safety, aggressive or violent behaviors, or other difficult to handle challenges associated with Sundown Syndrome, talk to your doctor about options. Vitamin therapies may also provide benefits, including vitamin B1 (thiamine) and vitamin D3. Vitamin B12 deficiencies are often recognized in the elderly. Some medications can interfere with the body's ability to absorb vitamin B, leading to not only fatigue, but depression, anxiety, and memory loss. In most cases, this can be dealt with through injections of vitamin B12.

7. Meet Basic Needs

Some symptoms of Sundown Syndrome can be alleviated by taking care of the basic needs of the individual. That means making sure that he or she gets adequate amounts of food, a light dinner, and focus on hydration.

8. Implement Redirection Techniques

Redirecting is a form of communication often utilized between Alzheimer's patients and caregivers. Redirection can mean many things including distracting, which is often effective in alleviating Sundown Syndrome behaviors such as repetition, pacing, and increased agitation. Caregivers and family members can be dealt with by asking yes or no questions in a calm manner. In addition, lightly touching and/or and maintaining a relaxed posture may also help, accompanied with direct eye contact and a smile.

Avoid arguing or trying to convince the individual experiencing Sundown Syndrome that things are not what they seem. Rather, empathize. An individual with Alzheimer's is often not thinking logically and does not follow the same sense of logic that a caregiver would. Confronting or arguing with such individuals only promotes a defensive reaction. Acknowledge what is concerning them, and then take steps to deal with it.

Relieving boredom, agitation, and repetitive questions can be dealt with by giving the person something productive and/or constructive to do. It does not matter whether they do it for five minutes or an hour. Engaging activities can help to relieve boredom that causes repetitive behaviors, and diverts focus and attention on something positive rather than negative.

71

9. Safety

Safety is essential when providing care for someone with Alzheimer's. Take steps to foolproof the home, reduce clutter, and redesign or re-situate things that a person dealing with visual problems may find confusing or frightening.

Chapter 8: The 7 Ways to Deal with Early Onset Alzheimer's/Dementia

Early onset Alzheimer's is defined as a type of Alzheimer's that occurs earlier in life than those over 65 (approximately 10% of individuals over 65 and roughly half of those over 85 are diagnosed with some type of dementia). Early onset Alzheimer's is defined as Alzheimer's that begins to affect someone in their 40s, 50s and early 60s. It is believed that early onset Alzheimer's or dementia may have a strong genetic link that may run in families. Contrary to most forms of dementia, early onset Alzheimer's occurs in about 5% of the population.

In order to deal with early onset Alzheimer's, it's important to recognize the most common signs and symptoms that may promote an early diagnosis. Like other stages of dementia, early onset Alzheimer's may be present in early, moderate, or late stages and effects individuals differently. As with other aspects of Alzheimer's it is always important to remember that this is not a one-size-fits-all disease process. The diagnosis affects different people in different and similar ways – whether dealing with early onset Alzheimer's or any of the stages of the disease as it progresses.

Many of us often forget things occasionally due to our busy lifestyles and obligations, but some of the earliest indications that something may be going on with a loved one is an increased difficulty in problem solving, multitasking, and in planning. Difficulties with concentration when dealing with too many things at once and confusion are relatively common. Managing financial affairs may also be difficult and quickly noticeable. It may become increasingly difficult to learn new information or to remember important dates.

An individual experiencing early onset Alzheimer's or dementia may also repeatedly ask for the same information and swear up and down that they have not asked you before. Such individuals may experience visual problems, and difficulty with depth perception is also common. A person with early onset Alzheimer's may also begin to experience poor judgment. Making decisions grows increasingly difficult. At this time, family members may begin to notice that judgment, decision-making, and reasoning/rationale skills are declining.

Dealing with Early Onset Alzheimer's

A number of steps can be taken by family members as well as caregivers to deal with early onset Alzheimer's or dementia. In such situations, reducing stress and excessive stimulation may help to reduce anxiety – beneficial for any stage of the disease. Keep in mind that at this stage of the disease process, the individual is perfectly aware that things are not "right" and may experience a wide range of emotions including everything from frustration to depression. In this section, I will provide a number of ways in which caregivers and family members can deal with early onset Alzheimer's.

1. Early diagnosis

The earlier a diagnosis is made, the more options a caregiver has for making plans or arrangements to deal with the future as well potential medications and therapies that may help slow the progression of Alzheimer's. Some of the most common tests utilized today to diagnose early onset Alzheimer's or other forms of dementia include but are not limited to computed tomography (CT) scans, and magnetic-resonance imaging (MRI) technologies.

In some cases, it is possible to see visual changes within the brain even at very mild stages of the disease. The MRI is capable of displaying any areas of atrophy in the brain.

A PET scan or a combination fluorofroxyglucose-positron emission tomography (FDG-PET) scan may also be recommended to determine if radioactive sugars are consistently metabolized in different regions of the brain. This test can diagnose a decline in metabolism of nerve cells, nerve connections, and synapses in the posterior or rear regions of the brain.

In addition, according to recent research and studies, it has been determined that individuals diagnosed with Alzheimer's have a high accumulation of a specific protein known as an amyloid in the brain. Newer tests using PET tomography that also utilize markers for this protein are also under development.

One of the earliest testing techniques that is performed (often in the doctor's office) in order to initially diagnose early onset or Alzheimer's is known as the Montréal Cognitive Assessment Test or MoCA. This test analyzes the intellectual capabilities of an individual and includes questions or directed tasks that determine memory capacity, language, and other reasoning and rationality skills. This test is also known as the Mini-Mental State Examination (MMSE), but is commonly utilized in testing for cognitive impairments following a vascular issue. This test can be especially beneficial in providing a diagnosis for vascular dementia.

The test provides a variety of tasks for an individual to complete. For example, the test includes visual spatial testing that requires the individual to draw an open cube, and provide directions for doing so. The individual is also directed to draw the face of a clock and then designate a time that indicates 10 minutes past 11. The second part of the test will require the individual to name a number of animals that are drawn on the test page. The third part of the test involves memory. For example, the doctor or the person giving the test will relate a short word list and the individual is asked to orally repeat the list back.

Following that is a short sequence of numerals that the person is asked to repeat in forward order, and then a shorter sequence of numerals to be listed backwards. Memory, attention, language, abstracts, and orientation are included in the test, which provides a score range for each task completed. A potential maximum of 30 points is achievable on the test, and anything above 26 points is determined as normal.

Diagnostic tests such as the aforementioned magnetic resonance imaging or MRI are often offered in conjunction with cognitive tests such as the Mini-Mental State Examination test.

Earlier diagnosis may aid in proactive measures including cognitive exercises and therapies coupled with drug therapies and other treatments that may help to slow the progression of early onset into the further stages of the disease process. There are no guarantees, however, that such efforts will be successful. Individual genetics as well as functions of those diagnosed with early onset may progress or remain stagnant based on individualized case scenarios.

2. Drug Therapies

John Hopkins recommends drug therapies that may enhance mental function. These medications include:

1. Aricept
2. Namenda
3. Excelon

In addition, antidepressants may be prescribed at this stage to help the individual deal with their diagnosis, which can trigger a variety of emotional mood swings. While results may be mixed, depending on individuals, such drug therapies may reduce the steady progression of the disease process by months or several years. I will talk more about drugs and medications in an upcoming section.

In a sense, a diagnosis of Alzheimer's, regardless of stage, can trigger a grieving process not only in the individual diagnosed, but in a spouse and other family members. In some cases, the emotional impact of an early onset or Alzheimer's diagnosis can provoke the same stages as it is experienced in a "traditional" grieving process. These stages may include:

- Denial
- Anger
- Bargaining
- Depression
- Acceptance

To a certain degree, an individual diagnosed with early onset Alzheimer's may experience these stages. There is no set time frame for the time it takes an individual to deal with any of these stages. Family members and most especially spouses should be aware of this, not only when it comes to their loved one's diagnosis with the disease, but with themselves.

3. Exercise

Physical activity enhances overall health and wellness and boosts circulation, balance, stamina, and coordination. Research is underway to study the effects of exercise and physical activity in slowing the progression of early onset Alzheimer's.

4. Diet and Nutrition

A well balanced and healthy diet rich in antioxidants will provide valuable support to the body during the early stages of Alzheimer's. The longer the body can maintain optimal physical function, development, and stasis, the more beneficial it is for the individual.

5. Cognitive Training

Cognitive training, otherwise known as "brain games" and exercises, may help to maintain cognitive abilities. Games or exercises that focus on reasoning and or rationalization, math problems, spatial awareness, and comparisons help to keep the brain stimulated.

Individuals experiencing early onset Alzheimer's are encouraged to find ways to maintain cognitive abilities by "exercising" the brain and providing stimulation by learning or trying new things and maintaining reasoning and problem solving skills.

6. Support

Support is especially important in families dealing with early onset Alzheimer's or other forms of dementia. Support from family, friends, and local groups as well as organizations provide not only emotional compassion and support, but also a wide variety of information, resources, and strategies for dealing with progressive stages and symptoms that present with Alzheimer's over time.

7. Prepare

Unfortunately, there is no cure for Alzheimer's. One of the best things you can do for the safety, comfort, and security not only of a loved one diagnosed with early onset Alzheimer's, but also for family members is to prepare and make decisions and arrangements during the early stages so that more difficult decisions and challenges in the future are made easier to deal with. A person experiencing symptoms of early onset Alzheimer's will still be able to make decisions, although such decisions should be made in conjunction with other family members whenever possible. For example, establish and make arrangements for future financial and/or health care decisions. Some of the things to consider include power of attorney in regard to finances and health care decisions.

Keep in mind that you or a loved one with early onset may experience up and down symptoms, and have some good days as well as bad days when it comes to making decisions and their immediate awareness of their condition. Be prepared to deal with bouts of irritability, depression, and anger in a person who is diagnosed with early onset.

8. Develop Daily Routines

Daily routines help reduce stress and confusion as much as possible. Offer help when you believe it is warranted, but otherwise try to encourage as much independence as possible in order to enhance a sense of self-esteem and quality of life in the individual. Even early on, routines can help reduce stress and anxiety and provide a calmer and more serene environment both at work (as long as the individual is able to continue working) as well within home environments.

9. Do Not Overcompensate

One of the most common situations that challenge those dealing with early onset Alzheimer's is that family members often try to overcompensate for their loved ones. This sometimes causes the person with early onset Alzheimer's to feel that he or she needs to be constantly monitored. This also increases stress not only for the individual involved, but in the overall family dynamic. As the diagnosis sinks in, the individual with Alzheimer's as well as family members will be able to better gauge what they are capable of doing and what they are not. Still, safety is and must always be a priority.

Even individuals diagnosed with early onset Alzheimer's or dementia may feel that they are perfectly capable of doing things, but because they may tend to forget or experience memory lapses, accidents can happen. This is especially true in situations that involve cooking. For this reason, it is best to supervise cooking sessions, and then make sure that ovens and stove tops or other appliances are turned off.

For individuals who insist on maintaining cooking skills or the ability to cook for themselves or family members, accessories that offer reminders may be beneficial. Timers that ding loudly to remind a person that something is on the stove or the oven is turned on, and so forth, are beneficial.

This may be a good point in time to go through the home and do what you can to make it a safer, more comfortable, and less stressful environment. The more you can do now to provide such an environment, the more comfortable and less stressful things will be as symptoms progress.

At the same time, keep in mind that early onset Alzheimer's may last for years before more serious symptoms appear, and individuals may go through this stage faster or slower than others.

Chapter 9: The 5 Common Drugs Used to Treat Sundown Syndrome

A number of medications are often prescribed in the treatment of symptoms of Sundown Syndrome and dementia. However, it's also important for caregivers to be aware that some medications can contribute to agitation and confusion, especially if a loved one is already experiencing symptoms of Sundown Syndrome. Some of these medications include antidepressants, anti-inflammatory medications, insulin, heart medications, and even some over-the-counter cold medicines.

When dealing with Sundown Syndrome and medications, talk to the doctor and make sure that he or she is aware of any and all medications (prescription, over-the-counter, herbal) that the individual is already taking. Before starting any new medication or therapy, discuss with the doctor to avoid interactions. Also be aware that too many medications may also exacerbate symptoms of Sundown Syndrome.

With that in mind, some of the most common drugs and medications prescribed in the treatment of Alzheimer's and Sundown Syndrome symptoms belong to the class of benzodiazepines. Some of the most common benzodiazepines provide anti-anxiety relief, and can include but are not limited to generic drugs like alprazolam (Niravan and Xanax), lorazepam (Ativan), and clonazepam (Klonopin).

However, recent studies have shown that benzodiazepines have been linked to an increased risk for Alzheimer's disease in those who have not yet been diagnosed. It is believed that a cumulative effect of benzodiazepines prescribed for anxiety and insomnia, especially long-term use, can increase this risk of developing Alzheimer's between 43% and 51% according to Medscape Medical News[6] in an article titled "Benzodiazepines linked to increased Alzheimer's risk."

It should be noted that many of the most common medications to treat Alzheimer's and symptoms of Sundown Syndrome treat the symptoms, and not the base cause of the symptoms in the brain. Some of these drugs are very difficult for a geriatric or aging brain to synthesize, so common practice is to try a medication for only a few months. If no positive effects are seen, it is recommended that the medications be stopped because continued for longer-term use may only exacerbate symptoms and create additional problems including those associated with negative behaviors.

According to the National Institute on Aging, cholinesterase inhibitors once commonly prescribed for treating the mild to moderate symptoms of Alzheimer's may no longer be recommended because they have led to exacerbation of behavioral problems.

Some of the newer generations of medications that are often prescribed to deal with mild to moderate symptoms include:

- Aricept - this drug is a cholinesterase inhibitor designed to prevent acetylcholine breakdown in the brain. Common side effects include diarrhea, nausea, and vomiting.

- Exelon - also a cholinesterase inhibitor, this medication is designed to prevent the breakdown of acetylcholine and butyrylcholine in the brain. This medication may not only cause nausea, vomiting, diarrhea, and weight loss, but loss of appetite as well as muscle weakness.

- Razadyne - also a cholinesterase inhibitor, this medication is designed to prevent the breakdown of not only acetylcholine, but to promote and release enhanced amounts of acetylcholine in the brain by stimulating nicotine receptors.

- Namenda - this antagonist is designed to block increase of toxicity and toxic effects associated with excessive synthesis of glutamate by regulating activation of glutamate in the brain. The most common side effects associated with this drug include headache, dizziness, confusion, and constipation.

It is only through studies (which can take years or even decades to accumulate data) that medical professionals can determine the efficacy of drugs and therapies designed to treat symptoms of Alzheimer's as well as its complicated issues. Where is the line between providing physical relief and worsening the potential for negative emotional behaviors. This aspect of research and treatment continues to face challenges. As a matter of fact, drugs often recommended in the past are no longer recommended today, or if prescribed at all are only done so for short periods of time in order to evaluate efficacy.

Risperadol has been used in the past to treat not only Parkinson's disease, but associated Alzheimer's disease symptoms that are often present in Parkinson's patients. However, Risperadol, also known as risperidone, an antipsychotic, causes blood pressure problems and is rarely prescribed anymore.

In the past, Cognix was also commonly prescribed for mild to moderate treatments, but is no longer recommended due to severe side effects which can include not only nausea and vomiting, but potential liver damage.

Tricyclic anti-depressants are not recommended and Haldol should only be used sparingly. These drugs often initiate or worsen negative behaviors that are not limited to severe anxiety reactions due to incessant wandering, vocal as well as physical abuse from patients directed toward their caregivers. This is especially challenging in home-based care scenarios where caregivers are most often family members and not trained professionals. In such situations, severe emotional trauma and even physical harm to caregivers is probable.

In the treatment of moderate to severe Alzheimer's, medications such as Namenda may be recommended. This antagonist (N-methyl D-aspartate) or NMDA may be somewhat effective in dealing the progression of symptoms in those diagnosed in the moderate to severe stages of the disease. This drug may help the individual maintain and perform daily functions, but its efficacy and ability to help for more than a few months is still under study.

Clinical trials are underway to determine the efficiency and safety of new treatments including anti-amyloid treatment in asymptomatic Alzheimer's disease. Other studies on immunoglobulin intravenous therapies that may be effective in mild to moderate Alzheimer's has just completed a Phase III study. In addition, another recently completed clinical study is attempting to

94

determine the effects of Rivastigmine patches (Exelon) in those with severe dementia in regard to their cognition and capability for performing activities of daily living.

Clinical trials regarding the efficacy of Verenicline (Chantix) on tolerability, safety, and cognition in those diagnosed with mild to moderate Alzheimer's is also underway, as well as the effects of other test medications including LY450139 and AZD3480.[7]

What does a nicotine patch like Chantix, or other medications that increase the stimulation of nicotine in the brain, have to do with Alzheimer's treatments? It is believed that nicotine enhances through the effect on specific nicotine cholinergic receptors in the brain, as well as in producing a variety of properties for antidepressant and anti-anxiety benefits. It is believed that the pathways between nicotine cholinergic and other specialty neurons including GABA, 5-HTP, dopamine, and norepinephrine may be beneficial in improving not only attention, but learning capabilities.[8]

Conclusion

Dealing with Sundown Syndrome or any aspect of Alzheimer's disease or dementia can be extremely challenging, not only on the individual experiencing the disease, but for family members and loved ones as well as caregivers. Understanding Sundown Syndrome and how it occurs is an important aspect of dealing with it. Understanding circadian rhythms and some of the most common symptoms associated with Sundown Syndrome are also important in helping caregivers as well as family members reduce triggers or circumstances that can lead to behavioral issues.

There is no prevention for Alzheimer's or its associated symptoms and behaviors – yet. However, one can reduce the chance of symptoms from developing by taking steps to eliminate those triggers that are most commonly recognized. Caregivers can help to adapt the environment as well as their own behaviors in order to cope with the challenging symptoms of Sundown Syndrome. Taking these steps in treating Sundown Syndrome as well as understanding common approaches, treatments and medications commonly used for mild to severe Alzheimer's stages is also important.

Dealing with any type of Alzheimer's diagnosis or dementia, including early onset Alzheimer's can be traumatic for all involved. However, information is power. I encourage anyone with a family member diagnosed with Alzheimer's to read as much as possible about the condition, its various stages, as well as the symptoms associated in these stages.

Sundown Syndrome can be extremely frustrating for caregivers and family to deal with, and finding coping mechanisms as well as support from family, friends, and public support groups can go a long way toward alleviating stress, frustration, and a sense of futility. Caregivers and family members need rest also. Caring for caregivers means taking time-outs, getting away from the caregiving situation once in a while, and not feeling guilty about doing so. The more rested you are, the better care you are able to provide.

Do what you can to safeguard the individual and provide a safe and comforting home environment. Foolproof the home and take steps to establish circadian rhythms that promote a clean delineation between awake and sleep patterns. Family members and caregivers will realize that no individual will react to the disease in the same way, and one must be willing to adapt and change direction when necessary. There is no specific way to approach a person experiencing Sundown Syndrome. At times, techniques like redirection or distraction will not work. In such cases, altering the physical environment, promoting exercise during the day, and rearranging scheduling of doctor's appointments and so forth may help to relieve and sometimes even alleviate some of the symptoms of Sundown Syndrome.

The key is education. Numerous organizations and support groups on the Internet are available, including the Alzheimer's Association and The National Institutes of Health, among other resources. Talk to your doctor about other resources and information available on the latest in clinical trials regarding medications and drug therapies that may help relieve symptoms, enhance memory, improve ability to complete activities of daily living as well as quality of life for a loved one.

Final Word/About the Author

I was born and raised in Norwalk, Connecticut. Growing up, I could often be found spending afternoons reading in the local public library about a variety of topics. It was from spending those afternoons reading about such an eclectic array of topics that I became highly interested in psychology and medicine. Usually I write works around sports to learn more about influential athletes in the hopes that from my writing, you the reader can walk away inspired to put in an equal if not greater amount of hard work and perseverance to pursue your goals. However, I began writing about topics such as Sundown Syndrome so that I could help others better understand how to cope with the development of different syndromes that sometimes come with age. If you enjoyed *Sundown Syndrome: The Ultimate Guide to What It Is, Treatment, and Prevention,* please leave a review! Also, you can read more of my general works on _ISTJs, INFPs, ENFJs, ENFPs, ISFPs, ISFJs, ESFJs, ESTJs, ESFPs, How to be Witty, How to be Likeable, How to be Creative, Bargain Shopping, Productivity Hacks, Morning Meditation, Becoming a Father,_ and _33 Life Lessons: Success Principles, Career Advice & Habits of Successful People_ in the Kindle Store.

Like what you read?

If you love books on life, psychology, or productivity, check out my website at claytongeoffreys.com to join my exclusive list where I let you know about my latest books. Aside from being the first to hear about my latest releases, you can also download a free copy of *33 Life Lessons: Success Principles, Career Advice & Habits of Successful People.* See you there!

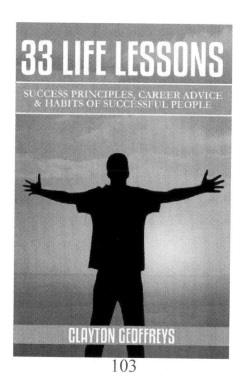

Endnotes

[1]Merck Manual of Medical Information – 2nd Edition

[2]"APOE." *Genetics Home Reference*, Lister Hill National Center for Biomedical Communications. Web. 2 Feb. 2015

[3]Foundations of Psychiatric Mental Health Nursing: A Clinical Approach - (Krahn, 2003; National Center on Sleep Disorders Research, 2003; Stickgold et al., 2004).

[4]"Circadian Rhythms Fact Sheet." *National Institutes of Health.* National Institute of General Medical Sciences, n.d. Web. 28 Jan. 2015

[5]Bryan, Derek. "From Sundowning to Insomnia: How Dementia Affects Circadian Rhythms." *Dementia.org.* Web. 24 June 2013

[6]Brauser, Deborah. "Benzodiazepines Linked to Increased Alzheimer's Risk". Medscape. Web. 09 Sept. 2014

[7]Clinical Trials.gov. A service of the U.S. National Institutes of Health. Web. 31 Jan. 2015

[8]"Varenicline and Alzheimer's Disease." *Psychiatry MMC* Online. US National Library of Medicine National Institutes of Health 2007 Dec; 4(12): 23-24 Web. Dec. 2007

Made in the USA
San Bernardino, CA
11 January 2016